THE ART OF GROWTH

The Yielding Warrior's Strategies for Thriving Martial Arts and Yoga Communities

Jeff Patterson

CONTENTS

1
INTRODUCTION

MY GOAL FOR THIS BOOK

Before we dive into the content, I'd like to outline the two primary goals that guided the creation of this book, *The Yielding Warrior Method*.

1. Immediate, Actionable Value

First and foremost, I aimed to ensure this book is immensely valuable to you. This means no fluff or filler.

Unlike many books you might find in major bookstores, which often include story after story to bulk up the page count, this book is different.

Here, you'll find concise, actionable advice specifically tailored for martial arts and yoga studio owners looking to build and expand their communities and profitability.

I've laid out clear strategies on how you can transform your business using the principles of *The Yielding Warrior Method*.

Every piece of advice can be immediately implemented to start seeing results.

Remember, acquiring knowledge through this book is just the first step; the real value comes from taking action on what you learn.

If you simply read and do nothing, you'll gain no advantage over someone who hasn't read the book at all. The strategies within have the power to change your business and life but only if you apply them.

2. Opportunity for Further Engagement: My second goal is to open doors to further collaboration.

Once you've seen the value in the pages of this book, and if you're impressed by the results you achieve, you might consider working with us further.

Throughout the book, you'll find opportunities to engage with my team and me.

Whether you take up that offer is entirely up to you, but executing the strategies is key.

In the field of business growth, particularly in niche markets like martial arts and yoga, there are countless 'experts' out there.

However, few truly offer something new or of substance.

Over the years, I've refined these strategies in real-world

applications, not only theorizing but also actively implementing them to build a thriving community and drive revenue in my own and others' studios.

This book is crafted to replicate that success for you, using a proven strategy that has already helped many studio owners.

If you find the strategies compelling and wish to implement them with expert help, I encourage you to reach out for a more tailored, effective engagement.

Whether it's through training, consulting, or complete done-for-you services, we're here to help you implement what you learn and achieve your goals.

Let's begin this journey with *The Yielding Warrior Method*, and transform your studio into a flourishing, profitable community.

WHO IS THIS BOOK FOR?

In the coming pages, you'll discover the exact methodology that has transformed our business more profoundly than any other strategy we've ever implemented.

The Yielding Warrior Method is not just another business manual it's a blueprint for those who are ready to make substantial changes in their lives and the lives of their clients.

If you aspire to enhance your expertise or acquire skills that can significantly benefit others, this book is designed for you. Whether you seek to refine your abilities or embark on learning a valuable new skill set, this guide is tailored to help you excel and make a positive impact on others.

If you possess immense ambition and are driven to create significant impacts in both your personal and professional life, this book is designed to guide you.

And crucially, if you're looking to streamline your business operations, clear the clutter of overcomplicated marketing strategies, and establish a straightforward system that consistently attracts your ideal clients, then you definitely need this book.

Over recent years, we've successfully applied *The Yielding Warrior Method* across a diverse range of fields, assisting coaches, martial arts studios, yoga studios, personal trainers, massage therapists, acupuncturists and service-based business owners in industries including:

- **Business**
- **Health & Fitness**
- **Mindset**
- **Leadership**
- **Academies**
- **Studios**
- **Life coaches**
- **Professional and amateur athletes**
- **Performers**

...and many more. Our experience spans over 30 years, and we've discovered that there isn't a single business in these industries that cannot benefit from integrating *The Yielding Warrior Method*, to develop well-crafted strategy to create a thriving community.

In essence, if you're dedicated to enriching your studio with a meditative arts program that consistently attracts and deeply impacts your clients—*The Yielding Warrior Method* will equip you with the precise strategies and insights needed.

This approach is designed to help you offer a transformative experience that not only enhances your clients' lives but also bolsters the growth and success of your business.

This book is your pathway to not just success, but meaningful, impactful success that resonates and creates a ripple effect of improvement and growth.

Let's embark on this transformative journey together.

PROBLEMS YOU'RE FACING

If you've been managing a martial arts or yoga studio for any period of time, you may have noticed that traditional methods of attracting and retaining clients are becoming less effective.

The issues you face today are unique to your industry and require a specialized approach to overcome.

Problem #1: High Turnover Rate - One of the most

persistent challenges is the high turnover rate of students, which can destabilize your business.

However, with *The Yielding Warrior Method*, we've maintained an exceptional retention rate, significantly outperforming our Brazilian Jiu Jitsu, Boxing, Muay Thai, and youth programs.

Our secret? A dedicated focus on long-term engagement that keeps students committed for over 30 years.

This method doesn't just teach techniques; it fosters a deep connection to the practice, making it an integral part of students' lives.

Problem #2: Not Utilizing Studio Downtime - Another issue is the underutilization of your studio during off-peak hours.

The demographic targeted by *The Yielding Warrior Method* typically older adults who often have flexible schedules that align perfectly with times when your studio is less busy.

By tapping into this group, you can maximize your space and resources, keeping your studio active and profitable throughout the day.

Problem #3: High-Cost Leads and Insufficient Traffic - The cost of acquiring new students can be prohibitively high, especially when competing for the most popular demographics.

However, *The Yielding Warrior Method* targets an often-overlooked audience, resulting in significantly lower lead costs due to reduced competition.

This approach not only decreases your marketing expenses but also increases traffic to your studio, making your advertising budget more effective.

Problem #4: Lack of Commitment to a Lifestyle Change - Finally, a common frustration is students' lack of commitment to a sustained practice or lifestyle change.

Our method addresses this directly by integrating the meditative arts deeply into the lives of our students, promoting a holistic approach to health and well-being that encourages long-term commitment and transformative life changes.

In the pages of this book, you'll find comprehensive strategies and actionable steps to overcome these problems using *The Yielding Warrior Method*.

This isn't just about keeping your doors open; it's about creating a thriving community where both students and business flourish.

We've successfully implemented these strategies across various niches within the wellness industry, proving time and again that our approach is not only viable but also highly effective.

By the end of this book, you'll have all the tools necessary to transform your studio, attract and retain the right clients, and significantly enhance both your professional and personal life.

DISCOVERY ASSESSMENT

Now, you likely have a sense of whether *The Yielding Warrior Method* resonates with your current needs and goals.

But before you dive deeper into this book, I encourage you to engage in the following business assessment exercise. It's designed to provide clarity on your studio's current standing.

You'll find a series of statements in the next few pages. For each statement, assign yourself a score from 1 to 5—where 1 is "not true at all" and 5 is "absolutely true".

Once you've responded to all the statements, sum up your scores. Refer to the scoring system provided below to accurately gauge where your business stands today.

If you're reading this book online, you can also take advantage of our digital version of this assessment.

Just click the link below. This online tool will automatically calculate your results and display them for you.

It's quick, easy, and completely anonymous—we don't require any personal information or opt-in.

Complete the Business Assessment Online

This exercise is an excellent first step towards understanding how well you are positioned to integrate and benefit from *The Yielding Warrior Method* in your studio.

Statement	Score (1-5)
I have more than enough clients and customers for my needs.	
My studio consistently attracts new students each month without any active advertising.	
I have a reliable system in place that ensures a steady flow of income from my studio.	
My marketing efforts require less than two hours per week to maintain.	
I use an evergreen system that consistently enrolls new students throughout the year.	
My current marketing funnel effectively covers all my advertising expenses upon first client acquisition.	
I gain a minimum of 30 new enrollments in my studio each month.	
I offer a high-value package or membership priced at $2,500 or more.	
My class schedule or appointment calendar is fully booked with committed students at least one week in advance.	
My studio's pricing structure is among the top 10% in the local market.	

Statement	Score (1-5)
I encounter minimal resistance when discussing enrollment options with potential students.	
My conversion rate for new student sign-ups is 75% or higher.	
I rely on one primary marketing strategy that consistently brings in qualified leads automatically.	
I have one streamlined marketing system that works effectively, eliminating the need for multiple strategies.	
Each month, I successfully meet or exceed my financial goals for the studio.	
I am confident in my ability to scale my studio's income to $100,000 per month or more.	
I have a competent and trustworthy team that helps achieve our studio's objectives.	
I can comfortably take 4–6 weeks of vacation annually, with my studio operating smoothly in my absence.	
I have ample personal time to enjoy with my family and for my personal interests.	

Statement	Score (1-5)
I find great satisfaction in working with the clients currently enrolled in my studio.	
I have a deep passion for running my studio and love my business.	
Total Score:	

WHAT YOUR SCORE MEANS

Score: 0–29
Fundamentals Are Missing

Unfortunately, your martial arts studio is lacking in several core areas essential for business success.

It's likely not a surprise, as these gaps probably cause quite a bit of stress.

The silver lining is that all is not lost.

You need to establish foundational systems, improve staff training, and implement effective student retention strategies.

As you explore this book, keep an open mind about how the strategies discussed could revolutionize your studio.

Imagine the potential transformation once you have these systems perfectly aligned.

You'll be amazed at how quickly you can turn things around once you apply the principles laid out in these pages.

Score: 30–69
Solid Ground, Ready for Growth

If you scored within this range, it indicates that while you have some systems in place, your studio's growth is hindered by ineffective marketing, inconsistent customer retention, or perhaps underdeveloped staff training.

You've made commendable progress, but you still lack a predictable system that facilitates rapid growth.

This book will guide you in refining your business model to not only attract but also retain a thriving community of students.

You'll learn how to leverage your offerings for maximum impact without needing to constantly generate new content.

Get ready to see a significant increase in committed students and experience what it truly means to have control over the growth of your business.

Score: 70+
Primed for Major Expansion

Congratulations! Your studio is on solid footing with a strong core offering and good operational practices.

Now, your challenge is scaling this success. You need systematic strategies for attracting new students and perhaps even expanding into new locations or offerings.

This book will introduce you to advanced strategies for scaling, using systematic approaches to marketing, student retention, and staff development.

You'll learn how to invest in growth initiatives confidently, ensuring that every dollar spent contributes to increased revenue.

If you're aiming to elevate your business into a major player

JEFF PATTERSON
result

within the martial arts community, the guidance found here will be invaluable.

Regardless of where you currently stand, this book has tailored advice to elevate your martial arts studio.

From hands-on training and mentorship to comprehensive

system overhauls, we're here to support your journey.

CHAPTER SUMMARY

The principles outlined in *The Yielding Warrior Method* are adaptable and highly effective, suitable for martial arts and yoga studios seeking transformational growth.

We've applied these strategies across numerous niches with outstanding success, proving that martial arts and yoga studios are no exception.

1. Strategic Foundations Over Lead Generation: In the martial arts and yoga studio industries, the challenge isn't generating leads; it's implementing the right strategies to attract and retain those leads. By establishing solid business systems, you ensure a steady influx of dedicated students.

2. The Limitations of Organic Marketing: Relying solely on organic marketing tactics like social media can be unreliable and slow. These methods lack the immediacy and control that more structured marketing strategies can offer.

3. The Power of Systematic Advertising: Paid advertising, when executed with a clear strategy, allows for predictable and scalable lead generation. With the right systems, your marketing efforts can consistently attract new students, allowing you to grow your revenue steadily.

4. Content Strategy and Student Engagement: Continuous content creation may seem beneficial but can overwhelm your audience and algorithms, reducing engagement. Instead, focusing on targeted, strategic content that aligns with *The Yielding Warrior Method* can build deeper connections with potential students, turning them into long-term participants.

By applying these tailored strategies, martial arts and yoga studios can not only attract more students but also enhance their operational efficiency, improve staff performance, and ultimately increase profitability.

This chapter sets the foundation for transforming your studio into a thriving community hub.

2

A JOURNEY BEGINS: THE GENESIS OF THE YIELDING WARRIOR METHOD

When I first opened the doors to my martial arts academy, I was driven by a deep passion for the arts and an earnest desire to share their transformative power with others.

What began as a small space focused primarily on Brazilian Jiu-Jitsu (BJJ), Muay Thai, and children's programs gradually expanded into something much greater a comprehensive center for physical and spiritual growth.

However, the road to success was neither straightforward nor predictable.

It was marked by significant challenges that tested my resolve and forced me to rethink my approach not just to martial arts, but to the business of running an academy.

THE EARLY STRUGGLES

For the first five to six years, my focus was almost exclusively on perfecting the craft.

I was determined to offer the best training in BJJ and Muay Thai, and I poured all my energy into coaching and improving my own skills.

My days were spent on the mats, teaching, training, and learning from every interaction with my students.

The children's programs were thriving because of the excitement and energy the kids brought with them, and the adult classes were filled with enthusiastic practitioners eager to learn.

However, despite the high level of engagement and the clear passion within the walls of the academy, the business side was suffering.

I had opened the academy out of a love for martial arts, naively neglecting the crucial elements of running a successful business. I was so immersed in the art that I ignored the art of business.

It wasn't long before the financial pressures of maintaining a space, managing bills, and ensuring enough student enrollment became overwhelming.

Revenue was inconsistent, growth was stunted, and the stress was palpable.

This stress was not just confined to financials but extended to the retention of students, who, despite their initial enthusiasm, often drifted away when the novelty wore off or when they felt they had reached a plateau in their training.

The Turning Point

The realization that my dream could very well collapse if I didn't make significant changes prompted a shift in focus.

Out of necessity, I started to delve into the business aspects of running an academy.

This shift was not easy; it required me to step back from the day-to-day teaching and invest time in learning how to manage and grow a business effectively.

I read books on business management, attended seminars, and even sought the counsel of successful academy owners who had navigated similar paths.

I began to understand that sustainability required a balance between passion for the craft and proficiency in business.

Incorporating the Meditative Arts

During this period of transformation, I introduced the meditative arts into our curriculum.

This decision came from a personal place I had experienced profound peace and focus in my own practice and wanted to share this with our students.

But from a business perspective, it was also a strategic move.

The meditative arts offered something that pure physical training did not a path to inner stillness and self-discovery that could retain students longer and deepen their commitment to the martial arts lifestyle.

The introduction of Tai Chi and Qigong, along with structured meditation sessions, added a new layer to our offerings.

These practices did not just complement the physical rigor of BJJ and Muay Thai but also provided a holistic approach to wellness that attracted a broader demographic.

Adults who were initially hesitant to join more physically demanding classes found a welcoming entry point through meditative arts.

Similarly, parents of children enrolled in our programs began to take classes themselves, drawn by the promise of stress reduction and improved mental clarity.

Business Growth Through Depth and Consistency

As the meditative arts became more integrated into our academy, I noticed a shift in the atmosphere and the business model.

These classes brought a consistency in attendance; people came for the physical benefits but stayed for the mental and emotional support these practices offered.

This retention was not incidental it was the result of creating a space that catered to comprehensive health, acknowledging and nurturing the connection between mind, body, and spirit.

The value of these programs was reflected in the financial stability they brought.

With higher retention rates, more consistent attendance, and an increase in family memberships, the academy began to see a more predictable and reliable revenue stream.

This financial stability allowed further investment back into the academy, enhancing facilities, expanding class offerings, and even allowing for the hiring of additional staff to enrich the student experience.

Lessons in Business and Passion

This evolution of the academy taught me a crucial lesson: passion needs to be supported by practical business strategies to create lasting impact.

While my initial years were driven by a singular focus on the arts, it was the balanced approach embracing the meditative alongside the martial that truly allowed the academy to thrive.

The journey of *The Yielding Warrior Method* is more than just a story of personal or business success; it's a testament to the transformative power of the meditative arts, both on the mat and in life.

As we continue to explore the development of this method, remember that its roots are deeply embedded in the challenges and solutions of those early years where every failure was a step towards greater understanding and every success a confirmation of the path chosen.

THE YIELDING WARRIOR METHOD FRAMEWORK

Embarking on the journey to transform my martial arts academy was driven by necessity and fueled by a profound dedication to the arts I practiced and taught.

However, the initial years of running the business highlighted a critical gap in my approach while I was deeply focused on the martial and meditative arts, I had underestimated the importance of robust business systems.

This realization was a turning point, leading to the development of *The Yielding Warrior Method* a structured framework designed to embed deep cultural, operational, and financial health into martial arts and yoga studios.

Step 1: Integrate the System into Your Business Model

The first step in adopting *The Yielding Warrior Method* is to integrate a comprehensive system into your existing business model.

For my studio, this meant a significant shift from a purely passion-driven operation to a balanced business approach that values both the art and the enterprise.

Initially, my focus was solely on the arts BJJ, Muay Thai, and children's programs dominated the curriculum.

However, the introduction of meditative arts such as Tai Chi and Qigong began to attract a broader demographic.

These disciplines brought not only new members but also stability and consistency to our business model.

To effectively integrate these systems, I had to learn and apply fundamental business principles that were previously foreign to me.

This included understanding market dynamics, customer retention strategies, and financial management.

Over the years, I invested heavily in my own education far exceeding the cost of traditional academic paths.

I attended masterminds, enrolled in courses, and sought mentorship, translating these learnings into systems that supported every aspect of the academy.

Step 2: Set Up a Funnel and Ad System

The second step focuses on establishing a marketing funnel and advertisement system that work seamlessly to attract and retain students.

In the early years, our marketing efforts were minimal, relying heavily on word-of-mouth and the intrinsic appeal of martial arts.

However, to grow and maintain our new offerings in meditative arts, a more structured approach was necessary.

I developed a funnel that begins with community engagement through workshops and free intro classes, which serve as an entry point for potential new students.

These initiatives were supported by targeted advertising campaigns that highlighted the unique benefits of integrating meditative practices with martial arts.

Our ads were designed to capture the interest of those seeking not just physical training but also mental and emotional well-being.

The effectiveness of this funnel was clear: it not only increased our leads but significantly improved our conversion rates.

By aligning our marketing strategies with the actual needs and interests of our target audience, we were able to reduce the cost per lead while increasing the lifetime value of each member.

Step 3: Create a Thriving Long-Term Community

The ultimate goal of *The Yielding Warrior Method* is to foster a thriving community that values lifelong learning and practice.

This doesn't happen overnight and requires consistent effort in cultivating an environment where members feel valued, supported, and motivated to continue their journey.

Community-building within the studio involved organizing regular events that encouraged social interaction outside of regular classes.

We hosted retreats, seminars with guest speakers, and family days that involved the members' wider circles, reinforcing the community aspect of our studio.

Moreover, we implemented mentorship programs within the studio where more experienced students would guide newcomers through their first months.

This not only helped new members integrate smoothly but also built a sense of loyalty and belonging, significantly boosting retention rates.

The focus on long-term relationships over short-term gains has established our studio as a pillar in the community a place where members know they are part of a supportive and nurturing family.

Moving Forward

As *The Yielding Warrior Method* continues to evolve, it remains rooted in the principles of balance between the art and the business of running a studio.

The framework is designed not just to attract members but to transform them into lifelong advocates of the practice.

Teaching them how to create an evolving life practice with the meditative arts and will produce endless fruits.

By embedding these systematic, thoughtful practices into the fabric of our operations, we ensure the sustainability and growth of our academy.

This journey from a struggling studio owner to a thriving community leader underscores the potential of *The Yielding Warrior Method* to transform not just businesses but lives.

As we delve deeper into the specifics of each step in the following chapters, remember that the core of this method lies in its holistic approach valuing the human element as much as the operational.

THE TWO ESSENTIAL OFFERS YOU NEED TO TRANSFORM YOUR STUDIO

Building a million-dollar business within the realm of martial arts and yoga does not necessitate a complex array of products and services.

Contrary to the common advice of needing a "value ladder" with varied offerings at different price points, achieving significant revenue growth can actually be much simpler.

To scale your business to consistently exceed $100,000 per month, you truly only need two key offers:

1. A Front-End Offer to capture leads
2. A Back-End Offer to deliver substantial value and revenue

Simplifying Your Strategy

Many studio owners get caught in the trap of believing they need to continuously create new programs and services to attract different types of customers.

This not only complicates the business model but also dilutes the focus from what truly generates substantial income.

Instead, by concentrating on just two strategic offers, you can streamline your operations and amplify your impact.

Front-End Offer: The Widget

In the context of *The Yielding Warrior Method*, the front-end offer isn't a book it's a widget.

This widget is a carefully designed tool that serves a dual purpose.

Firstly, it provides immediate value to potential students a taste of what your studio offers, perhaps through a free introductory meditation session or a trial Tai Chi class. Secondly, and most crucially, it captures essential contact information (email and phone number).

The beauty of this widget is that it's not just about giving something away for free; it's a strategic move to qualify leads and gather the necessary data to follow up effectively.

Once a prospective student interacts with this widget, their details are stored, allowing your team to reach out personally and invite them to a more detailed, in-person experience at your studio.

Back-End Offer: Comprehensive Membership Pro-

grams

Once leads are captured through the front-end widget, the next step is converting them into long-term members of your studio.

This is where your back-end offer comes into play.

Rather than just offering a basic class pass or single session fees, your back-end membership should be an extensive program focused on deepening the practice of your chosen path.

This membership should include comprehensive training modules that enhance both technique and lifestyle application, along with exclusive workshops and community events designed to fully integrate the discipline into a holistic lifestyle.

This high-ticket program is not just about attending classes; it's a holistic approach to personal development, wellness, and community building.

It's designed to transform casual attendees into committed members who see your studio as an indispensable part of their lives.

Operational Simplicity and Focus

By focusing on these two offers, you significantly simplify your business operations.

Your marketing efforts hone in on promoting the front-end widget, which leads seamlessly into your high-ticket, back-end offer.

This clarity not only enhances your operational efficiency but also improves customer experience by providing a clear and focused path from initial contact to deep engagement.

This strategic simplification does not mean sacrificing diversity in your offerings or failing to meet various customer needs.

Instead, it allows you to focus intensely on perfecting and scaling what truly works turning interested individuals into deeply engaged community members and driving predictable revenue growth.

By implementing this two-offer structure, you align your studio's operations with a proven business model that leverages both initial engagement and long-term commitment.

This approach ensures sustainability and growth, propelling your studio towards the million-dollar mark while maintaining the integrity and depth of your teachings.

THE FRONT END OF YOUR BUSINESS - THE YIELDING WARRIOR PROGRAM

The 'front end' of your business is crucial in setting the tone and expectation for potential new members.

It's everything that happens right up until someone becomes a paid member of your studio. In the context of *The Yielding Warrior Method*, we've crafted a highly attractive front-end offer to seamlessly draw in interested individuals and convert them into dedicated members.

Attracting Serious Students

The front-end of *The Yielding Warrior Method* isn't about casting a wide net with low-value offers; instead, it's about providing substantial value upfront to attract individuals who are serious about their personal development through martial arts.

Our front-end offer includes a free private introductory lesson, a complimentary uniform, and free access to all classes for 30 days.

This package not only introduces new members to the practice but also integrates them into the community, setting them on a path of commitment and deep engagement.

The Value of a Compelling Introductory Offer

The rationale behind such a generous introductory offer is multifold.

First, it breaks down barriers to entry, making it easy and risk-free for potential members to step into the world of the meditative arts.

Offering something as valuable as a private lesson and a uniform signifies a commitment to quality and student success, differentiating our program from others that may require upfront payment or commitment.

Second, this approach serves to immediately engage potential members in the culture and community of our studio.

By experiencing the personalized attention of a private lesson and the camaraderie of group classes, they can see the tangible benefits of becoming part of our community.

Liquidating Marketing Costs and Building Sustainable Growth

While offering free sessions and gear might seem costly, this strategy is designed to liquidate marketing expenses effectively.

Each person who signs up for the introductory offer represents a potential long-term member.

The initial cost is offset by the high conversion rate of trial members to paid memberships, thanks to the high-quality experience they receive.

Moreover, this initial engagement is not just about recovering costs but building a foundation for sustainable growth.

By providing exceptional value and a personalized experience from day one, we create a strong impression that keeps members coming back long after the trial period is over.

Establishing a Path to Premium Membership

The ultimate goal of this front-end strategy is to guide new members from their initial experience to premium membership offerings.

Throughout the 30-day trial, we showcase the depth and breadth of our program, emphasizing not only the physical benefits of martial arts but also the mental and spiritual growth that accompanies regular practice.

As members become more integrated into the studio's community and start experiencing personal transformations, the value of continuing beyond the trial becomes apparent.

This natural progression ensures that by the time the trial ends, members are ready and eager to commit to a longer-term engagement with us.

Next Steps in Optimizing the Front-End Strategy

As we move forward, our focus will be on refining and optimizing this front-end strategy to ensure that we continue to attract and retain motivated and dedicated members.

This involves continuously evaluating the effectiveness of our introductory offers and adjusting our approach based on member feedback and conversion rates.

In the following sections, we will explore how to leverage the initial engagement created by our front-end offer to build lasting relationships with members, ensuring that *The Yielding Warrior Method* not only attracts new students but also nurtures them into lifelong practitioners.

THE BACK END OF YOUR BUSINESS - THE YIELDING

WARRIOR PROGRAM

The concept of the 'back end' of your business refers to the processes and offers that come into play once initial contact has been established, often culminating in your main product or service.

For *The Yielding Warrior Method*, this involves transitioning from initial, low-threshold engagements to more substantial, long-term commitments.

Challenges with Direct High-Ticket Sales

Directly selling high-ticket programs to new or cold prospects can be highly inefficient and costly. The challenges are manifold:

1. High Customer Acquisition Cost: Selling expensive programs directly often entails significant upfront costs, which can severely impact the profitability of each sale.

2. Lack of Established Trust: New customers typically need time to build trust and familiarity with your brand before committing to a substantial investment.

3. Efficiency of Lead Qualification: Direct sales to cold leads have lower conversion rates and can lead to wasted resources.

Leveraging the Introductory Offer

In the context of *The Yielding Warrior Method*, instead of a book, we utilize the initial trial (comprising a free lesson, uniform, and

30 days of access) as our front-end offer.

This setup not only helps in qualifying leads by inviting a small commitment but also serves as a crucial relationship-building tool.

Through this initial engagement, potential members can experience the value of our community and the depth of our training without immediate pressure to commit to high-cost programs.

Transitioning to Premium Memberships

Once this relationship is established, we seamlessly guide these individuals towards our premium offerings.

Our back-end offer, a $2,400 12-month membership, provides a comprehensive and immersive experience, delivering extensive value that supports a deeper commitment from the members.

This membership includes structured progression in their chosen discipline, access to special workshops, and integration into community events, which enhances their engagement and retention.

Adding Value and Maximizing Profitability

While our primary back-end offer is substantial, the system is designed to be profitable on its own, each new member's acquisition costs are offset by their initial engagement, leading to a profitable escalation to higher levels of commitment without additional expenditure.

This approach ensures that the investments in advertising and marketing are recouped quickly, making the business model sustainable and scalable.

Optional High-Ticket Extensions

For studios looking to expand their offerings, considering additional high-ticket items could further enhance profitability.

For instance, special annual retreats, advanced personal development workshops, or certification programs for those who wish to teach can serve as lucrative high-ticket offers.

These should be tailored to the interests and capabilities of your members, ensuring they complement the existing programs and add distinct value.

Tailoring to Fit the Niche

While high-ticket items can significantly increase revenue, their success depends heavily on the specific niche and the perceived value they offer.

In the context of a martial arts or yoga studio, these offerings must resonate deeply with the member's goals and the community ethos to be effective.

In summary, the back end of your business in *The Yielding Warrior Method* is about deepening relationships and maximizing the lifetime value of each member through structured, meaningful engagement.

By carefully guiding members from introductory offers to premium memberships and potentially beyond, your studio can achieve sustainable growth and lasting impact.

CHAPTER SUMMARY

The Yielding Warrior Method redefines the process of building a profitable martial arts or yoga studio by focusing on two key offerings: a compelling front-end trial and a comprehensive back-end membership.

This method simplifies the business model into two main segments front-end and back-end streamlining the path to profitability and sustainability.

OVERVIEW OF THE YIELDING WARRIOR METHOD

1. **Introduce the Front-End Offer: The front-end of your business encompasses everything up to and including the first significant interaction or transaction.**

For *The Yielding Warrior Method*, this involves a free private introductory lesson, a complimentary uniform, and 30 days of free access.

This initial engagement is designed not just to attract interest but to facilitate a deeper connection with potential members, setting the stage for a longer-term relationship.

2. **Convert to Comprehensive Back-End Memberships: Following the front-end engagement, the back-end of the business focuses on converting those initial interactions into committed, long-**

term memberships.

Priced at $2,400 for a 12-month membership, this offer includes extensive training and community benefits that enhance the member's experience and commitment.

This is where the studio sees significant revenue growth and stability, as members invest in their health and wellness journey with the studio.

3. **Optional High-Ticket Extensions: While the primary focus remains on the foundational front-end trial and the back-end membership, additional high-ticket items such as annual retreats or certification programs can be integrated.**

These are designed to further enhance profitability and provide dedicated members with advanced opportunities for growth and engagement.

KEY BUSINESS INSIGHTS

- **Acquisition vs. Profit: A common error in business operations is attempting to profit from the initial customer acquisition phase.**

The Yielding Warrior Method emphasizes using the front-end offer as a means to effectively acquire new clients at low to no cost, thereby setting the foundation for profitability through the back-end membership.

- **Sustainable Business Growth: By separating the business into these two segments, it ensures a systematic approach to growing your studio.**

The initial free offers serve to attract and engage potential members, while the back-end membership drives revenue and deeper community integration.

- **The Role of High-Ticket Offers: While not essential, integrating high-ticket items can significantly boost a studio's revenue.**

These offers should be carefully considered to ensure they align with the needs and aspirations of the members, adding substantial value to their experience.

The Yielding Warrior Method is not just about financial growth but about creating a thriving community where members feel valued and engaged.

By following this structured approach, studio owners can transform their passion for martial arts or yoga into a flourishing business that impacts lives profoundly and sustainably.

3

THE ART OF INSTRUCTION: ESSENTIAL SKILLS FOR TEACHING MEDITATIVE PRACTICES

The Yielding Warrior Method offers a structured pathway to building thriving martial arts and yoga communities by emphasizing the development of an evolving life practice through meditative arts.

This program is designed to equip instructors with the tools needed to address a wide range of student goals, from health improvements to enhancing athletic performance.

KEY ELEMENTS OF THE YIELDING WARRIOR METHOD:

1. **Five Paths of Practice:**

   - **Athletic:** Focuses on enhancing physical abilities and sports performance through targeted exercises and mental conditioning.

   - **Therapeutic:** Uses meditative arts to address emotional and psychological well-being, helping to alleviate conditions like anxiety and stress.

   - **Medical (Qigong):** Applies traditional Chinese medical principles to improve health outcomes, addressing issues such as high blood pressure and chronic pain.

- **Philosophical:** Expands vision and strategic thinking, enabling practitioners to apply the wisdom of meditative arts in daily decision-making and life challenges.

- **Spiritual:** Encourages deeper self-awareness and connection to a higher purpose through disciplined spiritual practices.

2. Five Regulations:

- These are foundational principles that enhance the practice of meditative arts.

- Understanding and teaching these regulations can profoundly affect every aspect of a practitioner's life, providing a structured approach to personal growth and mastery of the discipline.

3. Teaching Competency:

- The program is structured to bring practitioners to a level of competency where they are confident in teaching beginners.

- It emphasizes the importance of a well-rounded approach that incorporates the technical, philosophical, and therapeutic aspects of meditative arts.

4. Continual Education:

- Stressing the importance of ongoing education, the program encourages instructors to deepen their knowledge and skills.

- This ongoing learning process ensures that they can offer increasing value to students at all levels of experience, from novices to seasoned practitioners.

5. Advanced Studies and Community Support:

- By staying connected with The Yielding Warrior community, members have access to advanced studies in meditation strategies, theory, and energetic principles.

- This network support ensures a vibrant learning environment that fosters both personal and professional growth.

This chapter lays the foundation for how instructors can utilize *The Yielding Warrior Method* to not only enhance their own practice but also to effectively guide their students through their individual journeys.

The program's comprehensive approach ensures that practitioners can meet a wide array of health, wellness, and performance goals, making it a pivotal addition to any martial arts or yoga studio looking to expand its impact and foster a deeply engaged community.

THE ATHLETIC PATH: ENHANCING PERFORMANCE THROUGH MEDITATIVE ARTS

In the realm of high-performance sports, the mental aspect of training is just as crucial as the physical.

The Yielding Warrior Method recognizes this interconnection and emphasizes the Athletic Path as a core component of its teachings.

This path is specifically designed to equip instructors with the strategies necessary to aid athletes in developing a robust mental skillset that complements their physical prowess.

Mental Skills for Athletic Excellence

The Athletic Path focuses on the cultivation of mental skills that are essential for high-performing athletes.

These include enhanced focus, improved concentration, stress management, and the ability to remain composed under pressure.

Such skills are often the differentiators between good athletes and great ones.

By integrating meditative practices into their training regimen, athletes can gain a significant advantage in competitive settings.

Focus and Concentration

One of the primary benefits of meditative practices for athletes is the enhanced ability to focus. In competitive sports, distractions are abundant.

The ability to remain focused on the task at hand, whether during practice or in the heat of competition, is invaluable.

Meditative techniques teach athletes to center their minds, eliminate distractions, and channel their energy towards achieving their immediate objectives.

Stress Management and Emotional Regulation

Athletes often face immense pressure, both from external expectations and internal ambitions. This stress can adversely affect performance if not properly managed.

Through the Athletic Path, practitioners learn to use meditative arts as a tool for stress management.

Techniques such as controlled breathing, mindfulness, and visualization help athletes regulate their emotions, maintain calmness, and approach their sport with a clear, unburdened mind.

Building Resilience and Mental Toughness

The path also focuses on building mental toughness, enabling athletes to persevere through setbacks and challenges.

Resilience is cultivated through practices that emphasize persistence, the acceptance of temporary failures as part of the journey, and the continual pursuit of improvement.

By regularly engaging in meditative practices, athletes can develop a thicker skin towards criticism and setbacks, viewing them as opportunities for growth rather than signs of defeat.

Application in Training and Competition

For coaches and trainers, understanding and implementing the strategies from the Athletic Path allows them to integrate these practices into regular training sessions.

This can be done through specific exercises that focus on mental visualization of success, meditation sessions aimed at enhancing self-awareness, and practices designed to improve the psychological stamina of athletes.

Incorporating these meditative practices into the daily routine not only prepares athletes for the physical demands of their sports but also equips them with the mental tools necessary to excel.

As athletes become more adept at managing their mental states, they can achieve higher levels of performance consistently.

The Athletic Path offered by *The Yielding Warrior Method* provides a comprehensive approach to athlete development, emphasizing the critical role of mental training in achieving sports excellence.

By mastering the meditative arts, athletes can unlock new levels of performance, making them more competent in handling the psychological demands of high-level competition.

For coaches, trainers, and athletes alike, investing in these skills is not just an enhancement of their physical capabilities but a fundamental shift towards a more holistic form of athletic preparation.

THE THERAPEUTIC PATH: CULTIVATING WELLNESS THROUGH MEDITATIVE ARTS

In the expansive realm of wellness and personal development, the therapeutic path of meditative arts offers profound benefits.

This approach focuses on healing and enhancing well-being through the intentional practice of mindfulness and meditation.

Understanding and implementing these strategies can significantly impact individuals seeking solace, healing, and mental clarity in their hectic lives.

Foundation of the Therapeutic Path

The therapeutic path in meditative arts is grounded in the belief that mental and emotional wellness is crucial for overall health.

This path teaches practitioners how to utilize meditation, controlled breathing, and mindfulness to address and alleviate various mental health issues such as anxiety, stress, depression, and chronic pain.

These techniques foster a deep sense of peace and well-being, making them essential tools for anyone involved in therapeutic practices.

Stress Reduction and Emotional Regulation

One of the primary benefits of this path is its ability to significantly reduce stress.

Through regular meditative practice, individuals learn to calm their minds, slow their thoughts, and focus on the present moment.

This mindfulness helps decrease everyday stress and anxiety by breaking the cycle of chronic worry and tension.

Additionally, these practices enhance emotional regulation, allowing individuals to better manage their emotional responses to external stressors.

The ability to remain calm and composed during stressful situations is invaluable, promoting a more balanced and resilient mental state.

Enhancing Focus and Mental Clarity

The therapeutic path also sharpens focus and mental clarity. In our fast-paced, often chaotic world, maintaining concentration can be challenging.

Meditative practices train the mind to focus intently on a single point of reference, such as the breath or a particular thought, without getting distracted by the noise of the environment.

This enhanced focus can then be applied to various aspects of life, improving efficiency and productivity at work, in relationships, and during leisure activities.

Recovery and Healing

For individuals recovering from physical or emotional trauma, meditative arts provide a gentle yet powerful healing tool.

Techniques such as guided visualizations and healing meditations can accelerate the body's natural healing processes and aid in emotional recovery.

These practices help individuals reconcile internal conflicts and overcome the mental barriers associated with past traumas, facilitating a journey back to wholeness and health.

Implementing Therapeutic Techniques

To effectively teach and implement these therapeutic techniques, instructors must first deeply understand and practice them.

This understanding allows instructors to empathetically and effectively guide their students through the nuances of meditative practice.

Instructors learn to create a safe, supportive environment where students can explore their inner landscapes without judgment, fostering an atmosphere of trust and openness essential for therapeutic work.

The therapeutic path within meditative arts is not just about teaching meditation; it's about equipping individuals with the tools they need to lead more emotionally and mentally balanced lives.

Whether dealing with daily stressors or more significant mental health challenges, the skills developed on this path can profoundly affect one's quality of life.

By fostering resilience, focus, and peace, the therapeutic path helps individuals build a foundation of inner strength that supports all aspects of their well-being.

THE MEDICAL PATH: HARNESSING QIGONG TO ENHANCE HEALTH THROUGH TRADITIONAL CHINESE MEDICINE

The medical path of meditative arts, particularly through the practice of Qigong, offers substantial health benefits rooted in the ancient wisdom of Traditional Chinese Medicine (TCM).

Qigong, a cornerstone of this path, combines movement, meditation, and controlled breathing to optimize the body's healing energy, known as Qi.

Understanding and teaching Qigong's principles can empower individuals to manage their health proactively, addressing both preventative and reactive health needs.

Qigong and Traditional Chinese Medicine

Qigong is an integral part of TCM, a holistic system that views the body as a network of interconnected energy pathways.

These pathways, or meridians, are responsible for the flow of Qi throughout the body.

According to TCM, health issues arise when there's a blockage or imbalance in this energy flow.

Qigong practices are designed to clear these blockages, enhance energy circulation, and, by extension, improve health and vitality.

Enhancing the Body's Natural Healing Abilities

One of the primary benefits of Qigong is its ability to enhance the body's natural healing capabilities.

By integrating slow, deliberate movements with deep, rhythmic breathing, Qigong helps to calm the mind and reduce stress, which is often a significant contributor to health issues.

The reduction of stress hormones in the body can lead to decreased inflammation, enhanced immune function, and increased stamina, all of which are crucial for maintaining physical health and recovering from illness.

Qigong for Chronic Conditions

Qigong is particularly beneficial for managing chronic health conditions such as hypertension, heart disease, and diabetes.

Regular practice can help regulate blood pressure, improve

cardiac function, and balance blood sugar levels.

Furthermore, Qigong's focus on gentle movement makes it accessible to individuals of all ages and physical abilities, including those who may not be able to engage in more strenuous forms of exercise.

Mental and Emotional Health

The benefits of Qigong extend beyond physical health, significantly impacting mental and emotional well-being.

The meditative components of Qigong encourage practitioners to focus inward, promoting a deep sense of peace and mental clarity.

This mental focus can alleviate symptoms of anxiety and depression, provide clarity in decision-making, and enhance overall emotional resilience.

The mindful aspect of Qigong teaches practitioners to live in the present moment, reducing the impact of past traumas and future anxieties.

Implementing Qigong in Health Practices

For healthcare providers and wellness instructors, integrating Qigong into their practice offers a non-invasive, cost-effective tool for patient and client health management.

Teaching Qigong requires a deep understanding of its principles and a commitment to the practice.

Instructors must be adept at guiding individuals through the movements and breathing techniques, ensuring they are performed with proper form and intention to maximize health benefits.

Moreover, instructors should be knowledgeable about the philosophies of TCM that underpin Qigong practices, enabling them to educate their students about how the exercises influence their health on a deeper energetic level.

This education is vital for motivating individuals to incorporate Qigong into their regular wellness routine, as understanding the why behind the practice increases adherence and engagement.

The medical path through Qigong offers powerful tools for enhancing health and wellness, grounded in the ancient traditions of Chinese medicine.

By teaching these practices, instructors provide their students with a holistic approach to managing their health, one that empowers them to take an active role in their well-being.

Whether addressing specific health conditions or enhancing general health and prevention, Qigong offers accessible, effective strategies that can profoundly affect all aspects of an individual's health.

THE PHILOSOPHICAL PATH: EXPANDING VISION AND

STRATEGY THROUGH MEDITATION

The philosophical path of meditative arts dives deep into the profound mental and intellectual benefits that meditation offers, particularly how it enhances strategic thinking and broadens perceptual awareness.

This path is not just about achieving temporary peace or relaxation; it's about cultivating a profound understanding of the mind's potential and applying this to all aspects of life.

Foundation of Philosophical Meditation

Philosophical meditation revolves around using meditative practices as tools for deep introspection and existential exploration.

This form of meditation encourages practitioners to engage with and question their core beliefs, values, and the very nature of their thoughts.

Through this introspective practice, individuals can achieve a clearer, more refined understanding of their purpose and the decisions that shape their lives.

Enhancing Strategic Thinking

One of the key benefits of philosophical meditation is its ability to enhance strategic thinking.

Regular meditation practice helps clear the mind of clutter and distraction, providing a cleaner slate for processing information and making decisions.

This heightened clarity allows individuals to consider various aspects of a situation more thoroughly, anticipate potential outcomes, and devise effective strategies.

In essence, philosophical meditation cultivates a form of mental agility and openness to new information, which is crucial for successful strategic planning and execution.

Expanding Peripheral Vision

In philosophical terms, expanding one's peripheral vision means developing an ability to be aware of more than the obvious, the immediate, or the expected.

Meditative practices train the mind to notice subtle details and patterns that might otherwise go overlooked. This expanded awareness can be particularly valuable in complex decision-making scenarios where the stakes are high and the outcomes are uncertain.

By enhancing one's peripheral vision through meditation, individuals learn not only to focus but also to maintain a broad awareness that can catch critical nuances of every situation.

Applying Philosophy in Practical Contexts

The philosophical path is not just about contemplation; it's about application.

The insights gained from deep meditative practice are meant to be applied in real-world contexts.

For instance, in a business setting, a leader might use meditative strategies to better navigate corporate politics or to innovate new business strategies.

Similarly, in personal relationships, this enhanced perception can lead to more empathetic interactions and more nuanced understanding of interpersonal dynamics.

Teaching Philosophical Meditation

Teaching this path requires a nuanced approach that not only instructs on the techniques of meditation but also on how to apply philosophical insights practically.

Instructors must be well-versed in various philosophical doctrines that underpin meditative practices and be able to guide students in applying these insights to enhance their professional and personal lives.

Philosophical meditation instructors thus act not only as guides in the techniques of meditation but also as mentors in the application of these techniques to complex real-world problems.

They help students develop a toolkit of mental strategies that can be applied to enhance decision-making and strategic planning in any area of their lives.

The philosophical path offers a rich, deep exploration of the mental capacities enhanced by meditative practice.

For anyone looking to deepen their understanding of themselves and the world around them, or to enhance their strategic abilities in any field of endeavor, this path provides both the theory and the practical techniques necessary.

By embracing the philosophical aspects of meditation, individuals can unlock new dimensions of their intellectual and perceptual capacities, leading to more insightful, strategic, and effective engagements with the world.

THE SPIRITUAL PATH: EXPLORING THE DEPTHS OF MEDITATIVE ARTS

The spiritual path of meditative arts transcends religious boundaries, offering a universal journey toward inner peace, self-awareness, and personal growth.

This journey is deeply personal, rooted in the exploration of one's inner landscape, and provides a profound understanding of the connection between the self and the broader universe.

Defining Spirituality in Meditative Arts

In the context of meditative arts, spirituality is understood as the quest for a deeper, intrinsic sense of meaning and connection with the essence of life.

It involves tapping into the innermost layers of consciousness and exploring the intangible elements that define our experiences and perceptions.

This path is not about adhering to specific religious doctrines but rather about seeking a personal truth that resonates with one's own experiences and worldview.

Cultivating Inner Peace and Harmony

One of the primary goals of following the spiritual path in meditative arts is to achieve a state of inner peace and harmony.

This is accomplished through practices that focus on mindfulness, deep reflection, and meditation.

These practices help individuals silence the incessant chatter of the mind, allowing for moments of profound quietude and clarity.

In these moments, practitioners often experience a sense of unity with their environment and a deep harmony within themselves, which can bring about lasting serenity and a reduced response to the stresses of everyday life.

Enhancing Self-Awareness

The spiritual path also emphasizes the cultivation of self-awareness.

Through consistent meditative practice, individuals learn to observe their thoughts, emotions, and reactions without judgment.

This heightened awareness fosters a deeper understanding of one's motives, fears, desires, and the subconscious patterns that dictate behavior.

With this knowledge, practitioners can begin to make more conscious choices in their lives, aligning their actions more closely with their values and aspirations.

The Journey of Self-Discovery

Engaging with the spiritual path in meditative arts is essentially a journey of self-discovery.

It encourages individuals to question and explore their own beliefs about the nature of existence, the purpose of life, and their personal role within the larger cosmos.

This exploration often leads to profound insights and transformative experiences that alter one's perception of self and other.

It's a journey that continuously evolves, offering new layers of understanding and connection as one delves deeper.

Non-Religious Spiritual Practices

The practices involved in the spiritual path of meditative arts are universal and can be adopted by anyone regardless of their religious background or lack thereof.

Techniques such as breath work, meditation, chanting (in a non-religious context), and guided visualization are used to foster a connection with the deeper aspects of the self and the universe.

These practices are designed to be inclusive, focusing on the human experience as a whole rather than on any specific theological doctrine.

The spiritual path of meditative arts offers a profound framework for personal growth and spiritual exploration outside the confines of organized religion.

It provides tools that help practitioners deepen their understanding of themselves and their place in the world, enhance their well-being, and live more harmoniously.

This path is not about finding answers in external sources but rather about discovering the truths that lie within each individual, leading to a more fulfilling and spiritually enriched life.

THE FIVE REGULATIONS: ENHANCING PRACTICE AND TEACHING IN MEDITATIVE ARTS

The Five Regulations in meditative arts serve as foundational principles that significantly enhance the practice and teaching of these disciplines.

Understanding and integrating these regulations can deepen one's own practice and substantially increase the value provided to students.

These regulations Body, Breath, Mind, Qi, and Spirit are interconnected and work synergistically to promote a comprehensive approach to personal and spiritual growth.

1. Regulation of the Body

The first regulation involves proper alignment and relaxation of the body.

In meditative practices, maintaining a posture that supports ease and stability is crucial.

This involves understanding the mechanics of the body and how to position it in ways that enhance energy flow rather than restrict it.

For practitioners and instructors, mastering body regulation means being able to maintain physical composure in meditation and movement practices, which is essential for achieving deeper states of meditation and higher efficiency in performing physical tasks.

By teaching students how to regulate their bodies, instructors empower them to practice more effectively, reducing the risk of injury and increasing the benefits of practice.

2. Regulation of the Breath

Breathing is a vital aspect of life and meditative practices.

Regulation of breath involves controlling and optimizing breathing patterns to enhance energy flow and mental concentration.

Proper breathing not only oxygenates the blood and maintains physical health but also calms the mind and prepares it for deeper meditative states.

Instructors who teach breath regulation help students manage their physiological and psychological responses to stress, enhancing their capacity for relaxation and focus.

This skill is particularly valuable as it provides students with tools they can use both within and outside of meditative sessions.

3. Regulation of the Mind

The mind can be the most challenging aspect to regulate due to its tendency to wander and hold onto patterns of overthinking and rumination.

Regulation of the mind involves training it to remain present and focused, avoiding distractions from past concerns or future anxieties.

Mastery of mind regulation allows practitioners to achieve deeper levels of meditation and insight, unlocking profound levels of inner peace and mental clarity.

When instructors guide students in mind regulation techniques, they are equipping them with the ability to control their thoughts and emotions, which is invaluable in all areas of life.

4. Regulation of Qi

Qi, or life force energy, is a central concept in many Eastern philosophies and medical theories.

Regulation of Qi involves practices that enhance the circulation of this vital energy throughout the body.

Techniques might include specific movements, breathing exercises, and mental focus that guide Qi along the meridians or energy pathways.

A clear understanding of how to regulate Qi can lead to improved health, vitality, and a greater sense of well-being.

Instructors who are adept at teaching Qi regulation can help their students overcome energetic blockages and harness their energy more effectively, which is especially beneficial for health and vitality.

5. Regulation of Spirit

The regulation of spirit refers to cultivating a state of harmony and alignment with one's higher self or true nature.

This regulation is about connecting with the deeper aspects of one's being and the universe.

It involves practices that foster a profound sense of connectedness and purpose, contributing to spiritual growth and existential satisfaction.

Instructors who incorporate spirit regulation into their teaching

THE ART OF GROWTH

help students find greater meaning in their practices and lives, facilitating transformative experiences that extend beyond the physical and mental benefits of meditative arts.

The Five Regulations are essential for developing a deeper and more effective meditative practice.

They not only enhance personal practice but also enrich the teaching process, allowing instructors to offer a more holistic and impactful experience to their students.

By mastering these regulations, practitioners and instructors alike can provide immense value, helping students to achieve balanced growth across physical, mental, energetic, and spiritual dimensions.

Thus, understanding and applying the Five Regulations is fundamental to advancing in the meditative arts and fulfilling the role of a competent and compassionate instructor.

EMPOWERING INSTRUCTORS: BUILDING COMPETENCE AND CONFIDENCE IN THE YIELDING WARRIOR METHOD

The Yielding Warrior Method is meticulously designed to elevate practitioners to a competent level, ensuring they possess the necessary skills and confidence to deliver true value to their students.

This comprehensive approach is focused on fostering a deep understanding of meditative arts and their applications, enabling instructors to guide their students effectively through their own journeys of personal and spiritual growth.

The core of the program revolves around a structured curriculum that covers the theoretical and practical aspects of meditative arts.

This includes an in-depth study of the Five Regulations Body, Breath, Mind, Qi, and Spirit each integral to mastering the art of meditation and teaching it effectively.

By gaining a profound understanding of these elements, practitioners are equipped to address a wide range of needs and aspirations, enhancing their ability to tailor their teachings to individual students.

Moreover, the program emphasizes practical experience through hands-on training and real-world application.

Instructors are given numerous opportunities to practice teaching under the guidance of experienced mentors, receiving constructive feedback that hones their instructional techniques and interpersonal skills.

This practical training is crucial for building confidence, as it allows future instructors to experience first-hand the dynamics of leading a class, managing different personalities, and adapting their teaching methods to various learning styles.

Additionally, *The Yielding Warrior Method* stresses the importance of continuous learning and personal practice.

Instructors are encouraged to maintain their own meditative practices and pursue further education in advanced concepts and techniques.

This commitment to personal and professional growth not only deepens their own practice but also ensures they remain knowledgeable and relevant in their teachings.

By the end of the program, participants are not just competent; they are confident, well-equipped, and inspired to teach.

They emerge as leaders capable of making a significant impact on their students' lives, armed with a comprehensive toolkit that allows them to deliver profound and lasting value.

This level of preparation is what sets *The Yielding Warrior Method* apart, making it a transformative experience for both instructors and their future students.

CONTINUAL EDUCATION: LIFELONG LEARNING WITH THE YIELDING WARRIOR METHOD

In the dynamic field of meditative arts, the landscape of knowledge and techniques is ever-expanding.

Recognizing this, *The Yielding Warrior Method* emphasizes the crucial role of continual education in the development of its instructors.

This commitment to lifelong learning ensures that instructors can deliver increasing value to their students, catering to everyone from novices to advanced practitioners.

Deepening Knowledge and Skills

The Yielding Warrior Method offers a structured pathway for instructors to deepen their understanding of meditative arts.

It provides advanced training sessions that cover new research, techniques, and teaching methodologies.

This ongoing education is vital for instructors to keep their skills sharp and their knowledge current, allowing them to remain effective educators as the fields of meditation and martial arts evolve.

Modular Learning Approach

The program adopts a modular learning approach, where instructors can progressively build on their existing knowledge without feeling overwhelmed.

Each module is designed to introduce more complex concepts and practices that build on the fundamentals taught in earlier stages.

This methodical approach to learning ensures a solid foundation of skills that can be continually expanded and refined.

Integration of Latest Research and Practices

Staying abreast of the latest research in psychology, physiology, and neurology as they relate to meditative practices is another critical component of the program.

The Yielding Warrior Method integrates these insights into its curriculum, providing instructors with a deeper understanding of how meditative practices affect the mind and body.

This knowledge allows instructors to adapt their teaching strategies to be more effective and responsive to the needs of their students.

Community Learning and Peer Collaboration

A significant aspect of continual education within *The Yielding Warrior Method* is the emphasis on community learning and peer collaboration.

Instructors are encouraged to participate in regular workshops, retreats, and online forums where they can share experiences, challenges, and insights with their peers.

This collaborative environment fosters a sense of community and provides a supportive network where instructors can learn from each other and grow together.

Access to Advanced Courses and Certifications

Finally, *The Yielding Warrior Method* offers access to advanced courses and certifications for those instructors who wish to specialize further or move into new areas of practice.

These opportunities not only provide additional learning but also enable instructors to diversify their teaching portfolios, attracting a broader range of students and meeting the community's evolving needs.

In conclusion, continual education is a cornerstone of *The Yielding Warrior Method*, ensuring that its instructors are well-equipped to provide high-quality, up-to-date instruction.

By investing in the ongoing development of its instructors, the program not only enhances the personal growth of the teachers themselves but also significantly enriches the learning experience for their students.

Advanced Studies and Community Support in the *Yielding Warrior Method*

The Yielding Warrior Method recognizes the importance of continual growth and community in the journey of mastering meditative arts.

To support this, the program offers extensive opportunities for advanced studies and fosters a strong community network that enhances both personal and professional development for its members.

Access to Advanced Meditation Strategies

Members of The Yielding Warrior community have the unique opportunity to delve deeper into sophisticated meditation strategies that go beyond foundational practices.

These advanced techniques, which might include progressive stages of mindfulness, deep meditative states, or complex visualizations, are designed to enhance mental clarity, emotional stability, and energetic balance.

By exploring these advanced strategies, practitioners can expand their own practice and gain new insights and techniques to bring into their teachings.

Theoretical Understanding and Energetic Principles

Along with practical techniques, the program emphasizes a profound theoretical understanding of the meditative arts.

This includes studies on the philosophical underpinnings, historical contexts, and the latest scientific research related to meditation and its effects.

Additionally, the program explores the energetic principles that govern the practice of meditative arts, such as the concepts of Qi or Prana and their impact on health and wellbeing.

This holistic education allows instructors to deepen their expertise and offer more nuanced guidance to their students.

Vibrant Community Support

The Yielding Warrior community is a vibrant network of practitioners and instructors who share a common passion for meditative arts.

By staying connected with this community, members gain the invaluable benefit of peer support and knowledge sharing.

The community organizes regular meet-ups, workshops, and seminars that provide platforms for members to connect, share experiences, and learn from each other.

This continuous interaction fosters a supportive learning environment that is vital for both personal growth and professional development.

Personal and Professional Growth

The community and the advanced studies provided by *The Yielding Warrior Method* are integral to the personal and professional growth of its members.

Instructors who engage regularly with the community and participate in advanced studies find themselves better equipped to handle the challenges of teaching and more adept at adapting their methods to meet the needs of their students.

Furthermore, the ongoing education and community support help to prevent professional burnout by keeping the practice fresh, inspiring, and deeply connected to the evolving landscape of meditative arts.

Advanced studies and community support are cornerstone features of *The Yielding Warrior Method*, ensuring that practitioners continue to grow and thrive within their practices.

These opportunities not only allow members to deepen their knowledge and skills but also to become part of a dynamic network that values continuous learning and mutual support.

The combination of advanced studies and a supportive community thus serves to greatly enrich the personal and professional lives of all members, propelling them towards greater achievements in both their practice and teaching of meditative arts.

CHAPTER SUMMARY: STRATEGIES FOR THRIVING MARTIAL ARTS AND YOGA COMMUNITIES

This comprehensive chapter explores a multifaceted approach to enhancing martial arts and yoga communities through the integration of meditative arts.

Each section delves into a unique aspect of meditative practice, outlining methods and philosophies that enrich both personal practice and instructional prowess.

The Athletic Path: Enhancing Performance through Meditative Arts

This section highlights how meditative practices can significantly boost athletic performance by improving mental focus, physical endurance, and recovery rates.

It discusses specific meditative techniques that athletes can use to sharpen their competitive edge and maintain psychological resilience.

The Therapeutic Path: Cultivating Wellness through Meditative Arts

Focusing on the healing potential of meditative arts, this part examines how meditation can alleviate stress, anxiety, and physical ailments, thereby enhancing overall wellness.

It offers practical insights into integrating these therapeutic practices into daily routines for health benefits.

The Medical Path: Harnessing Qigong to Enhance Health through Traditional Chinese Medicine

This segment explores the integration of Qigong and Traditional Chinese Medicine principles into meditative practices.

It explains how Qigong promotes health by balancing the body's energy systems and enhancing the natural healing processes.

The Philosophical Path: Expanding Vision and Strategy through Meditation

Delving into the intellectual benefits of meditation, this section discusses how meditative practices can expand cognitive boundaries and enhance strategic thinking.

It provides strategies for applying philosophical insights to improve decision-making and problem-solving skills.

The Spiritual Path: Exploring the Depths of Meditative Arts

This part focuses on the spiritual dimensions of meditative practices, emphasizing personal growth and existential exploration.

It discusses how deep meditation can lead to profound insights and a heightened sense of connection with the universe.

The Five Regulations: Enhancing Practice and Teaching in Meditative Arts

Exploring foundational principles vital to the practice and teaching of meditative arts, this section breaks down the Five Regulations Body, Breath, Mind, Qi, and Spirit.

It illustrates how mastery of these elements can significantly enhance the effectiveness and depth of both personal practice and teaching.

Empowering Instructors: Building Competence and Confidence in the *Yielding Warrior Method*

This segment addresses the training and development of instructors within *The Yielding Warrior Method*.

It emphasizes the importance of a solid educational foundation and practical experience in building instructor competence and confidence.

Continual Education: Lifelong Learning with the *Yielding Warrior Method*

Highlighting the importance of ongoing learning, this part discusses the opportunities for continued education within The Yielding Warrior community.

It shows how perpetual learning is crucial for keeping teaching methods fresh and effective.

Advanced Studies and Community Support in the *Yielding Warrior Method*

Finally, this section explores the advanced studies and community support available through *The Yielding Warrior Method*.

It describes how these resources provide a supportive and enriching environment for both personal and professional growth.

Together, these sections provide a detailed roadmap for practitioners and instructors looking to deepen their understanding and enhance their skills in the meditative arts, ultimately leading to thriving martial arts and yoga communities.

4

THE ART OF CONVERSION: TURNING PROSPECTS INTO DEDICATED MEMBERS OF THE YIELDING WARRIOR PROGRAM

THE POWER OF A FOCUSED SQUEEZE PAGE WITH A COMPELLING WIDGET

In the digital marketing landscape, capturing leads and efficiently converting them into appointments and eventually paying members are crucial for business success.

A well-designed squeeze page, particularly when equipped with a compelling widget, is often more effective for these purposes than a traditional website.

This efficiency stems from the focused nature of squeeze pages, designed specifically to capture leads through a clear, concise, and highly targeted approach.

Focused Call-to-Action

A traditional website contains a wealth of information, including details about various programs, history, staff bios, and more.

While informative, this abundance of information can distract potential leads from taking immediate action.

In contrast, a squeeze page simplifies the user's decision-making process by focusing solely on a single call-to-action (CTA).

For instance, our widget prompts visitors to enter their name, email, and phone number to schedule a free private lesson, receive a free uniform, and enjoy 30 days of free training upon membership.

This direct approach eliminates distractions and leads visitors towards one specific action, enhancing the chances of conversion.

Immediate Engagement

Squeeze pages are designed to engage users the moment they land on the page.

The absence of navigational options ensures that visitors are not wandering around the site but are instead immediately presented with an attractive offer.

Our widget leverages this by offering tangible benefits upfront, which captures interest and incentivizes action.

By providing clear value a free lesson, uniform, and training period we address the visitors' potential needs and desires right away, making it easier for them to decide in favor of giving their contact information and scheduling an appointment.

Higher Conversion Rates

Thanks to their straightforward layout and targeted content, squeeze pages typically enjoy higher conversion rates compared to traditional websites.

They are crafted to lead a visitor down a single pathway, significantly reducing the bounce rate that can occur when visitors are presented with too many options.

Additionally, the specific nature of the offer and the ease of the sign-up process via the widget ensure that the leads captured are of higher quality.

These are individuals who have already expressed a significant interest in the academy by opting into the specific offer.

Streamlined Follow-Up Process

With a traditional website, capturing lead information often requires navigating through multiple pages or searching for contact forms, which can lead to potential clients dropping off before completing the process.

A squeeze page with a widget simplifies this process tremendously.

Once a prospect fills out the widget form, their information is immediately available for follow-up.

This quick access allows for rapid engagement, increasing the likelihood of converting an interested visitor into an appointment.

The faster response times can make a substantial difference in customer acquisition efforts.

Testing and Optimization

Another significant advantage of using a squeeze page over a traditional website is the ease of testing and optimizing.

Squeeze pages can be easily modified to test different elements like headlines, CTAs, images, and more to see what converts best.

This testing leads to continually improved results and a better understanding of what motivates your target audience to act.

The data gathered from these tests can help refine marketing strategies and improve the overall effectiveness of the campaign.

In conclusion, a squeeze page with a compelling widget is a superior tool for capturing leads and scheduling appointments compared to a traditional website.

Its focused approach, immediate engagement with visitors, higher conversion rates, streamlined follow-up process, and ease of optimization make it an essential element of digital marketing strategies for businesses like martial arts academies.

By effectively harnessing the power of a well-crafted squeeze page, businesses can maximize their lead capture efforts and significantly boost their membership conversions.

THE ART OF SETTING APPOINTMENT CALLS: A CRUCIAL FIRST CONTACT

When setting up appointments for martial arts or yoga classes, the initial call isn't just a logistical interaction; it's the foundational step in building a relationship with a potential new member.

This call is often the first real point of contact between your business and the customer, so handling it with care and attentiveness can significantly impact the success of your program.

To optimize this crucial interaction, it's important to engage with potential clients in a manner that reflects the quality and dedication of your academy.

Establishing a Connection

Think of the appointment-setting call as a first date.

You're not just informing; you're engaging.

This means taking the time to genuinely connect with the caller, going beyond the surface to understand their motivations and needs.

Begin the conversation by welcoming them warmly and expressing genuine interest in their inquiry.

Example Script Start: "Hello! Thank you for calling [Academy Name]. This is [Your Name] speaking. How can I assist you on your journey with us today?"

Discovering Their Interests and Goals

Once initial pleasantries are exchanged, steer the conversation towards understanding what specifically attracted them to your program.

Ask open-ended questions to encourage them to share more about themselves. This not only helps in tailoring the conversation but also builds rapport.

Example Questions:

- "What sparked your interest in our training program?"
- "Are there specific goals you're hoping to achieve with martial arts/yoga?"
- "Do you have any previous experience, or are you starting a new journey with us?"

Uncovering Deeper Motivations

Often, the surface reason someone gives for joining a class is just the tip of the iceberg.

Probing deeper into their motivations can reveal more about their true aspirations, which can help you better address their needs.

This understanding can guide you to recommend the right programs and create a personalized experience from the outset.

Example Probing Questions:

- "That sounds like a great goal! Besides achieving [stated goal], is there something more you're hoping to gain from martial arts/yoga?"

- "What does success in this training look like to you personally?"

Educating and Expanding Their Vision

Once you've established a connection and understand their goals and deeper motivations, use the opportunity to educate them about aspects of the practice they might not have considered.

Share 2-3 insights about how your practice can enrich their life, tying these back to the interests and goals they mentioned.

Example Educational Insights:

- "Based on what you've told me about your interest in improving focus, you might find our mindfulness practices particularly beneficial.

They're designed not just to enhance physical agility but also to sharpen mental clarity."

- "Many of our members have found that beyond just physical health, the techniques we explore can significantly improve stress management and personal growth."

Setting the Appointment

With a strong connection established and their interest piqued by new insights, it's time to set the appointment.

Emphasize that their chosen instructor is reserving a full hour to dedicate to them, underscoring the personalized attention they will receive.

Example Transition to Scheduling: "I'd love to schedule a time for you to meet with [Instructor's Name].

They're really looking forward to exploring these aspects with you and have reserved an hour to focus entirely on your needs."

Finalizing Details

Conclude the call by confirming all logistical details like the academy's location, parking information, and anything else they need to know.

It's crucial to end the call with a request for a courtesy call if they need to reschedule, ensuring you maintain a high level of professionalism and respect for your staff's time.

Example Closing: "Before we finish, can I ask you to call us at least 24 hours in advance if you need to reschedule?

This allows us to offer your slot to someone else and helps us maintain a great learning environment for everyone. Does that work for you?"

Handling the appointment-setting call with this level of care not only sets the stage for a successful first lesson but also begins to weave the fabric of a long-term relationship.

By the end of the call, the potential new member should feel valued, understood, and excited about the journey ahead with your academy.

This approach transforms a routine interaction into a powerful engagement tool, paving the way for higher show rates and committed members.

GREETING AND PRE-LESSON LOGISTICS: SETTING THE TONE FOR SUCCESS

Creating a welcoming and organized environment from the moment a new member walks through the door is crucial in establishing a positive first impression and setting the tone for their experience with your academy.

The initial greeting and the steps that follow are designed to make newcomers feel valued, comfortable, and well-informed.

Immediate and Warm Greeting

The first rule of engaging new members is never to let them feel unacknowledged. Greet each person warmly within 30 seconds of their arrival.

This prompt greeting is vital to making them feel expected and welcome. An excellent greeting might go like this:

"Hello, welcome to [Academy Name]! My name is [Your Name], and I'm so glad you're here. I'll be right with you to introduce you to your instructor."

This initial interaction should be genuine and inviting, providing the newcomer with immediate recognition and a sense of belonging.

Setting Them Up Comfortably

After the initial greeting, guide the new member to a comfortable waiting area.

This could be a simple gesture but it significantly enhances the visitor's comfort, especially if they are feeling nervous or unsure about the new environment.

During this time, inform them about where they can place their belongings, such as a bag or jacket.

This not only helps in keeping the space organized but also assures them that their personal items are taken care of:

"You can hang your jacket here and place any bags in this area. Please have a seat over here while I get the form you'll need to fill out and fetch your instructor."

Information Sheet and Waiver

Hand them an information sheet and a waiver to fill out.

This document should gather essential details such as their

name, contact information, goals for joining the academy, any previous training they've had, and an emergency contact.

The goal section is particularly important as it helps the instructor tailor the session to meet the visitor's expectations.

It's crucial to ensure that your waiver is legally sound.

Utilizing tools like GPT for drafting the initial document can be incredibly beneficial for structuring and articulating the terms clearly.

However, having a local attorney review the document is essential to ensure that it meets all legal requirements and effectively protects your business:

"While you fill this out, I'll go and inform your instructor that you're ready. If you have any questions about the form, feel free to ask when I return."

Seamless Transition to the Lesson

Once the new member completes the form, ensure that the transition to meeting their instructor and starting the lesson is smooth and swift.

The instructor should be ready to greet them personally, thank them for the information provided, and begin their tour or lesson:

"Thank you for filling out the form. Here's [Instructor's Name], who will be working with you today.

They'll start by showing you around and then you'll begin your lesson. Enjoy your time with us!"

The steps from the initial greeting to the start of the lesson are designed to establish a foundation of trust and professionalism.

By managing these pre-lesson logistics effectively, you not only enhance the new member's comfort but also demonstrate the organized and caring nature of your academy.

These first interactions are pivotal in turning first-time visitors into long-term members, setting the stage for a successful and enriching experience at your martial arts or yoga studio.

CONDUCTING A TOUR AND PRIVATE LESSON TO CONVERT PROSPECTIVE STUDENTS

When introducing potential students to the unique atmosphere and philosophy of your academy, the initial tour and private lesson are crucial touchpoints that can significantly influence their decision to join.

With years of refining this process, I've developed an approach that consistently achieves high conversion rates, ensuring that about 85-90% of visitors decide to enroll.

Here's a detailed guide on how to replicate this success in your own academy.

Initial Greeting and Comfort

First impressions are lasting.

Begin with a warm, personal greeting as soon as the prospective student enters your academy.

Make sure to address any initial concerns such as parking and directions immediately, which helps in setting a relaxed tone.

Asking if they have prior experience in any related disciplines not only gathers information but also provides a personal touch, showing genuine interest in their background.

Introducing the Concept and Paths of Practice

Once comfortable, introduce them to the core concepts behind your teachings.

Explain the different paths they can embark on within your meditative arts program.

For instance, outline the athletic, therapeutic, medical, philosophical, and spiritual paths, highlighting how each can enrich their practice and align with their personal goals.

This segment of the tour is not just informative but also illustrative of the depth and versatility of your program, catering to a variety of interests and needs.

Setting Expectations and Commitment

It's crucial to set clear expectations about the commitment required to benefit from the program. Emphasize the importance of regular practice, suggesting a manageable routine such as 20 minutes a day.

This conversation sets the stage for commitment, making it clear that while your program is profoundly beneficial, it requires consistent effort and dedication.

THE TOUR: ENGAGING THE PROSPECTIVE STUDENT

During the tour of your facility, keep the conversation flowing by pointing out areas where different activities take place.

Use this opportunity to introduce the philosophical underpinnings of your practice, perhaps stopping to discuss a piece of artwork or an inspirational quote displayed prominently.

This part of the tour is not only about showing the physical space but also about embedding the prospective student into the culture and ethos of your academy.

Demonstrating the Value of Your Practice

After the tour, begin the private lesson by demonstrating simple but fundamental exercises.

These should illustrate the basic principles of your practice, such as awareness, balance, and breathing.

For instance, start with basic Tai Chi movements or simple breathing exercises that underscore the mind-body connection.

This hands-on experience is vital as it allows the prospective student to feel the immediate benefits of the practice, such as relaxation and increased body awareness.

Deepening the Experience

As you guide them through the exercises, take the opportunity to expand their understanding and appreciation of the practice.

Explain how these initial exercises are the building blocks for more advanced practices and how they integrate into daily life for improved health and well-being.

This approach helps the student visualize a pathway of progression and personal development within your academy.

Closing the Lesson and Membership Enrollment

Conclude the lesson by revisiting the benefits they've just experienced and discussing how the academy can support their goals through structured classes and community support.

Invite them to view the class schedule and select times that fit their routine, guiding them through the membership options.

This is the moment to present the membership package, detailing the benefits and the community they will be joining.

Ensure that this process doesn't feel rushed; continue to add value by talking about the community and the ongoing support they will receive.

Assure them that they have made a great decision, emphasizing the transformative potential of their journey with your academy.

Finally, after they sign up, it's crucial to continue the engagement rather than ending with a quick goodbye.

Reinforce their decision by highlighting upcoming events or classes where they can start their journey, and ensure they feel welcomed into the community.

This ongoing engagement helps solidify their commitment and enhances their integration into the academy's culture.

By meticulously planning and executing each step of the tour and private lesson, you create a welcoming and informative experience that showcases the depth and value of your academy, significantly increasing the likelihood of converting prospects into committed students.

ONBOARDING NEW MEMBERS: ENSURING A SMOOTH START

The transition from prospect to active member in any martial arts or meditative arts academy is a critical phase.

This period shapes the new member's perception of the academy, impacts their initial experiences, and influences their long-term commitment.

To ensure this transition is smooth and sets the foundation for a lasting relationship, a structured approach to the first few classes and ongoing communication is essential.

Here's a detailed guide on how to effectively integrate new members into your program, from scheduling to ongoing support.

Effective Communication and Scheduling

Once a new member has signed up and chosen their class times, the immediate next step is to confirm these classes with a confirmation text.

This message should be sent the morning of the class or the day before if the class is scheduled for the morning.

This communication is not merely a reminder; it serves as a reiteration of your commitment to their journey in martial arts or meditative practices.

It helps reduce no-shows and reinforces the member's decision to join by maintaining high engagement from the outset.

Personalized Welcome

On the day of their first class, ensure that the instructor is well-prepared to receive them.

This preparation involves more than just knowing the new member's name.

Instructors should be briefed on any relevant information the member shared during their introduction tour and private lesson such as their goals, any previous experience, and particular interests or needs they may have expressed.

This knowledge allows the instructor to provide a personalized welcome and creates a connection from the very beginning, making the new member feel valued and recognized.

Instruction and Integration

The first class is a pivotal moment for new members.

It is not just an introduction to the physical aspects of the practice but also an orientation to the culture and community of your academy.

It's important that the instructor outlines what a typical class entails and integrates the new member with the existing group seamlessly.

During this first session, the instructor should teach the foundational exercises or forms that the new member will be practicing at home.

This immediate integration of learning and practice helps the new member feel equipped to start their home practice, reinforcing the lessons learned in the academy and enhancing their confidence in executing the techniques independently.

Home Practice Support

Home practice is a crucial component of the learning process in any discipline that involves physical and mental training.

During the initial classes, the instructor should emphasize the importance of daily practice at home and explain how it ties into their progress and achievement of goals.

Instructors should provide clear, manageable routines that new members can follow outside the academy.

This guidance should be practical, precise, and tailored to the individual's level, ensuring they feel capable of carrying out the exercises on their own.

Follow-Up and Engagement

After the first class, follow-up is key to retention and member satisfaction.

Instructors should check in with new members to ask about their home practice.

This follow-up can be through a phone call, a text message, or a brief conversation before or after their next class.

These check-ins serve multiple purposes: they show the member that their progress and well-being are important to the academy, they provide an opportunity for the member to ask questions or express concerns, and they reinforce the habit of regular practice.

The instructor's involvement doesn't end with technical training; it extends into ongoing support and encouragement.

By actively engaging with new members about their practice and progress, instructors can quickly address any challenges and help integrate new members into the community more deeply.

Long-Term Integration

As new members become more comfortable and adept in their practice, instructors should continue to guide them towards deeper involvement with the academy.

This might include inviting them to special workshops, introducing them to more advanced classes, or involving them in community events.

Each of these steps helps to weave new members into the fabric of the community, ensuring they feel a part of something larger than just a class they attend.

By taking these steps, academies can ensure that new members are not only well-integrated into the physical practice and community culture but also supported in a way that promotes long-term engagement and satisfaction.

This approach helps in building a loyal and committed member base, critical for the sustained success of any martial arts or meditative arts academy.

CHAPTER SUMMARY: OPTIMIZING MEMBER ACQUISITION AND ONBOARDING IN MARTIAL ARTS AND YOGA STUDIOS

This section of the book focuses on effective strategies for converting prospects into committed members of martial arts and yoga studios, outlining a clear, structured pathway from the first point of contact through to full integration into the community.

The Power of a Focused Squeeze Page with a Compelling Widget

This chapter explores the importance of designing a squeeze page specifically tailored to capture leads effectively.

It discusses how a well-crafted widget, offering tangible incentives like a free private lesson, uniform, and additional trial period, can significantly increase conversion rates by providing immediate value and a clear call to action.

The Art of Setting Appointment Calls: A Crucial First Contact

Appointment setting is more than just arranging a time for a prospective member to visit; it's an opportunity to build a connection and understand their needs and goals.

This chapter details how to conduct these calls in a way that sets the stage for a long-term relationship, using techniques that involve deep listening, engaging questions, and educational elements that position your studio as the solution to their needs.

Greeting and Pre-Lesson Logistics: Setting the Tone for Success

First impressions are crucial.

This chapter covers the best practices for welcoming new visitors to your studio, from the immediate, warm greeting upon their arrival to the logistics of their visit.

It includes tips on making them feel comfortable, informed, and prepared as they begin their first lesson, ensuring they feel valued and respected from the moment they walk in the door.

Conducting a Tour and Private Lesson to Convert Prospective Students

A detailed guide on how to conduct a tour and private lesson that maximizes the potential for converting prospects into paying members.

This chapter breaks down the steps to demonstrate the value of the program effectively, leveraging both the physical facilities and the philosophical underpinnings of the practice to solidify the prospect's commitment to join.

Onboarding New Members: Ensuring a Smooth Start

The final chapter in this section focuses on the critical steps to properly onboard new members after they have signed up.

It emphasizes the importance of effective communication, personalization of their initial experiences, and the integration of these new members into the community.

Strategies include scheduled follow-ups, personalized training sessions, and the continuous engagement that fosters a sense of belonging and commitment.

Each chapter is designed to build upon the previous, creating a comprehensive strategy that ensures every prospective student not only signs up but becomes a lasting and engaged member of your community.

5

MASTERING THE ART OF PAID TRAFFIC: A GUIDE TO FILLING YOUR FUNNEL

OPTIMIZING AD SPEND FOR THE YIELDING WARRIOR PROGRAM: TARGETING A UNIQUE DEMOGRAPHIC

When expanding your Yielding Warrior Program, utilizing paid advertising becomes even more compelling due to the unique demographic it targets individuals aged 50 to 80.

This focus not only differentiates your program from typical martial arts and yoga classes geared towards 20-40 year olds or children but also presents a strategic advantage in advertising cost efficiency.

Cost-Effective Advertising for an Older Demographic

1. *Less Competition:* The market for targeting the 50-80 age group is considerably less saturated compared to the more commonly targeted younger demographics.

Fewer businesses vie for their attention, especially in the realm of physical and meditative practices, leading to lower advertising costs.

2. *Higher Engagement:* Older adults tend to have more stable lifestyle patterns and are often looking for meaningful ways to enhance their health and overall well-being.

As a result, they are more likely to engage deeply with content that speaks directly to their interests and needs, such as the health benefits and community aspects of *The Yielding Warrior Method*.

3. *Greater Ad Visibility:* Platforms like Facebook, which provide detailed targeting options, often show lower cost per click (CPC) rates for audiences that are less targeted by the mainstream advertisers.

This demographic not only sees fewer ads but also may respond more positively to ads that directly address their specific interests, such as lifelong health, community involvement, and personal growth.

4. *Higher Conversion Rates:* Due to their mature nature and more deliberate decision-making processes, older adults are likely to consider their investments carefully.

Once they decide to engage with a program like the Yielding Warrior, they're more committed and likely to follow through, leading to higher conversion rates from ad impressions to actual program participants.

Strategic Implications for the Yielding Warrior Pro-

gram

By focusing your advertising efforts on this older demographic, you can significantly reduce your customer acquisition costs.

The savings can be redirected to enhance program features or to increase reach within the same budget, maximizing the impact and growth of your program.

Moreover, this approach aligns perfectly with the ethos of *The Yielding Warrior Method*, which prizes depth of engagement and personal growth, qualities that resonate strongly with an older audience.

This strategic alignment not only improves financial outcomes but also enhances the authenticity and appeal of your brand.

Building a Sustainable Growth Model

Leveraging the cost advantages of targeting an older demographic allows for a more sustainable growth model.

You can achieve more predictable and stable growth by reaching an audience that is not only more likely to engage but also more appreciative of the depth and continuity offered by *The Yielding Warrior Method*.

In conclusion, when you tailor your paid advertising strategy to target the 50-80 year-old demographic for *The Yielding Warrior Method*, you tap into a unique market segment that offers lower ad costs and higher engagement rates.

This strategic focus not only enhances the efficiency of your marketing efforts but also aligns with the core values of your program, ensuring that every dollar spent is an investment in building a thriving, committed community.

BUILDING BLOCKS FOR EFFECTIVE ADS

Writing effective advertisements is both an art and a science.

It's about understanding the psychological triggers of your audience and presenting your offer in a way that resonates deeply with their needs and desires.

The process isn't about random creativity but rather about assembling specific elements to build a compelling message that prompts action.

Let's break down these elements and explore how they form the foundation of successful advertising.

1. The Hook/Problem

The hook is your ad's opening statement and arguably the most critical part of your ad copy.

It's what catches the eye or ear of your potential customer and pulls them into the narrative you're creating.

This could be a question, a startling statistic, or a bold statement that addresses a specific problem that your audience faces.

The effectiveness of your hook directly influences whether someone will continue engaging with your ad or scroll past it.

2. Pain Points

Identifying and articulating the pain points of your target audience is crucial.

These are the specific problems or frustrations your prospects experience in their daily lives that your product or service can solve.

Highlighting these pain points not only increases relevance but also builds an emotional connection, making the prospect feel understood and more open to the solution you offer.

3. Solution/Story

After presenting the problem and agitating the pain points, introduce your solution.

Your product or service should appear as the natural answer to the problems highlighted.

Detail how your solution works and why it's effective, ideally positioning it as a unique or superior choice compared to others on the market.

4. Benefits/Bullet Points

While features are an important aspect of your offering, benefits convey the real value to the consumer.

Benefits answer the crucial question, "What's in it for me?"

Transform features into benefits that directly impact the user's life, work, or happiness.

Use bullet points for clarity and ease of reading, ensuring that each benefit is compelling and straightforward.

5. Authority

Establishing credibility is vital in convincing your audience that you and your solution are trustworthy.

Incorporate elements of authority such as expert endorsements, certifications, awards, or media mentions.

Customer testimonials can also serve as powerful indicators of authority and trustworthiness.

6. Curiosity

Keeping some information back can be just as important as the information you provide. Curiosity leads to higher engagement rates.

Crafting your message in a way that piques interest without giving everything away can encourage your audience to click through to learn more.

7. Call-to-Action (CTA)

A clear, compelling call-to-action is essential for converting interest into action.

Your CTA should be direct and instructive, such as "Sign up today," "Book your free trial," or "Get started now."

It should also be easy for the customer to act upon. The positioning of the CTA in the ad copy is crucial—it should be placed prominently after establishing value.

8. Risk Reversal

Address potential objections by including risk reversal elements like money-back guarantees or free trial periods.

These offers reduce the perceived risk for the customer and can significantly increase conversion rates by providing a safety net.

9. Desires

Connect with the deeper desires of your audience.

Whether it's achieving success, finding peace, improving health, or gaining recognition, tapping into these intrinsic motivations can make your ad resonate on a more personal level.

IMPLEMENTATION IN PRACTICE

For instance, when crafting an ad for *The Yielding Warrior Method*, you might begin with a hook that taps into a widespread issue among potential clients, such as chronic stress from daily life.

Describe pain points like the ongoing battle against stress and the ineffectiveness of temporary solutions.

Then, introduce The Yielding Warrior as a comprehensive method that not only helps manage stress but also cultivates a deeper sense of mental peace and resilience.

Highlight benefits such as reduced stress levels, increased emotional stability, and a nurturing community that supports each member's journey.

Establish credibility by mentioning the years of experience behind the program and sharing testimonials from long-standing members who have seen significant improvements.

Spark curiosity by teasing some of the unique stress-reduction techniques that members can master.

Conclude with a compelling call-to-action, inviting viewers to sign up for a free introductory session to start their path to a more peaceful life.

By understanding and using these building blocks, you can assemble ads that not only capture attention but also convert viewers into loyal customers.

Like any skill, proficiency in ad writing improves with practice and experimentation, allowing you to refine your approach based on real-world feedback and results.

INTRODUCING THE 'MIRROR AND MULTIPLY' ADVERTISING STRATEGY FOR THE YIELDING WARRIOR PROGRAM:

When managing online ads, it's easy to get overwhelmed by countless variables. Yet, in reality, most of these details aren't critical.

Here's a streamlined approach to our advertising campaigns tailored for *The Yielding Warrior Method*:

Firstly, we develop several variations of our ad.

It's wise to test multiple ads rather than just sticking with one, increasing your chances of hitting upon an effective message.

We then launch these ads targeting specific audiences with a daily budget of $10.

For those with larger budgets, it's feasible to set up multiple ad sets to test different audiences, but ensure only one audience is targeted per ad set.

For beginners, focusing on a single, well-defined interest often yields the best results.

We let the ads run for a few days to allow spending and performance stabilization. Using our scaling calculator, we determine the acceptable cost per acquisition.

After the initial run, we assess the performance:

- If an ad is underperforming and costing more than it

returns, we shut it down.

- If an ad breaks even or profits, we duplicate it.

This duplication results in two identical ad sets, each with a $10 daily budget.

This method helps us avoid the pitfalls of directly increasing an ad set's budget, which can unpredictably affect its performance.

By duplicating successful ads, we can increase exposure and engagement without altering the original successful setup, allowing the proven ads to continue performing well.

Providing the funnel and back-end offer of The Yielding Warrior are well-optimized, this 'Mirror and Multiply' strategy effectively scales advertising efforts.

It supports the growth of the program towards a million-dollar enterprise without the risks typically associated with increasing ad budgets abruptly.

CHAPTER SUMMARY: OPTIMIZING AD SPEND FOR THE YIELDING WARRIOR PROGRAM: TARGETING A UNIQUE DEMOGRAPHIC

This chapter delves into strategic approaches for optimizing advertising expenditures tailored to the unique demographic of 50-80-year-olds.

This age group often offers cheaper ad costs compared to the more commonly targeted 20-40-year-olds.

By focusing on this demographic, *The Yielding Warrior Method* can effectively reduce its customer acquisition costs while still engaging a receptive and underserved audience.

Building Blocks for Effective Ads

Effective advertising is not about luck but about assembling key components in a strategic way to build a compelling message.

This section breaks down the essential elements of successful ads, such as creating a strong hook, addressing pain points, highlighting benefits, and incorporating a clear call to action.

These elements form the foundation for ads that not only capture attention but convert viewers into members of *The Yielding Warrior Method*.

Introducing the 'Mirror and Multiply' Advertising

Strategy for The Yielding Warrior Program

The 'Mirror and Multiply' strategy is a novel approach to digital advertising specifically tailored for *The Yielding Warrior Method*.

By mirroring successful ads and then multiplying their reach through careful scaling, this method allows for controlled growth in ad spend while maintaining or improving return on investment.

This strategy ensures that the program reaches more potential members without compromising the quality of engagement or inflating costs.

Each section of this chapter provides actionable insights and practical methods for turning a routine advertising effort into a powerhouse channel for growth, ensuring that *The Yielding Warrior Method* not only reaches its intended audience but does so in a cost-effective and efficient manner.

6
NEXT STEPS

THE END RESULTS

Transform your martial arts or yoga studio into a flourishing enterprise with the *Yielding Warrior Method*. This strategic approach allows you to effectively:

1. **Steady Growth:** Establish a reliable system that consistently attracts 20-40 new members each month, focusing on providing a tailored experience that resonates with the unique needs of martial arts and yoga practitioners.

2. **Customized Instruction:** Deliver high-quality, personalized instruction that adapts to the individual goals and abilities of each member, ensuring they derive the maximum benefit from your programs.

3. **Efficient Conversion Funnel:** Implement a conversion funnel specifically designed for martial arts and yoga studios, which efficiently turns interested individuals into dedicated members of your community.

4. **Optimized Sales Process:** Utilize a streamlined sales strategy that effectively introduces new students to the core practices and philosophies of your studio, guiding

them towards a deep and committed engagement.

5. **Impactful Community Building:** Create a nurturing environment that fosters not just physical and mental well-being, but also spiritual growth and community connection among your members.

If these goals resonate with you, it's time to focus your efforts.

Simplify your client acquisition by integrating the *Yielding Warrior Method* into your studio's strategy.

This approach consolidates your marketing efforts into a single, powerful strategy that reflects the depth and value of your offerings, ensuring your studio not only grows but also becomes a pivotal part of your members' wellness journey.

NEED GUIDANCE?

Achieving success in the realms of martial arts and yoga requires three critical steps:

1. **Knowledge** – In this guide, I've shared with you the necessary knowledge to create and launch the *Yielding Warrior Method*, alongside a robust funnel system designed to scale your martial arts or yoga studio to new heights.

2. **Decision** – By choosing this program, you've already taken a significant step toward success. Many who delve into these pages are already thriving in their respective fields and recognize the potential of implementing a specialized program to attract their ideal clientele.

3. **Action** – It's time to act. Statistics suggest that many people abandon their goals even before taking the initial step toward achieving them. Stand apart from the average and move forward with determination.

If you're contemplating whether to embark on this journey independently or seek assistance, consider this:

My team and I are here to facilitate the seamless integration of the *Yielding Warrior Method* into your business, ensuring efficiency and success.

Schedule a consultation with us at https://calendly.com/jeff-theyieldingwarrior/the-yielding-warrior and let's tailor a strategy that best fits your studio's needs.

During our consultation, we will review your business model in detail and provide you with a clear, actionable plan tailored to your martial arts or yoga studio.

We offer a range of support options, including comprehensive training programs that guide you through each step.

Leverage my 36 years of experience to elevate your business. Let's achieve growth and success together. It would be our privilege to help you achieve similar success. Whether we collaborate or you choose to proceed on your own, the key is to begin now.

Don't let this opportunity slip through your fingers. Take that decisive step towards enhancing your studio and enriching your community.

Act today, and perhaps in the near future, we can meet to discuss how the *Yielding Warrior Method* has transformed your business and your life. I look forward to the possibility of celebrating your successes together.

Wishing you all the success in the world,

Jeff Patterson, Founder of the *Yielding Warrior Method*

LIKE THESE IDEAS?

We'd like to thank you for your support with a free copy of *The Yielding Warrior*. Dig deeper and develop an evolving life practice with this book, packed with the tools, strategies, and structure you need to find success, develop healthier relationships, and become your best self.

Visit the link below to claim your free copy:

https://book.theyieldingwarrior.com/free-plus-shipping

www.ingramcontent.com/pod-product-compliance
Lightning Source LLC
Chambersburg PA
CBHW070927270326
41927CB00011B/2757